A Hallelujah Day
The Adventures of Madame Flutterby
Book 1

Written and Illustrated by Linda Fulford Gault

AuthorHouse™
1663 Liberty Drive
Bloomington, IN 47403
www.authorhouse.com
Phone: 1-800-839-8640

First published by AuthorHouse 05/19/2011

ISBN: 978-1-4634-1419-1(sc)

Printed in the United States of America

Any people depicted in stock imagery provided by Thinkstock are models,
and such images are being used for illustrative purposes only.
Certain stock imagery © Thinkstock.

This book is printed on acid-free paper.

Dedication Page

I dedicate this book to Almighty God
and thank Him for giving me the joy in writing
and illustrating as He directs.

To my dear younger brother, Charles Fulford, who went home to be with the Lord 12/17/10. Your generous love and kindness published this book, this ones for you.

To Douglas Spurr. My dear friend, although you were taken from us much to young, you will never be forgotten.

I dedicate this book to all the women in my life. You have embraced me and given me so much love with your friendships. Special thanks to The Purple Bag Ladies, strangers brought together in love for a moment in time.

Thank you, Jim MacDonald, for your understanding friendship, laughter and encouragement to write.

It was a glorious morning. Madame Flutterby called it a Hallelujah Day...so quiet and still, even the birds were whispering their cheerful good morning song so they wouldn't disturb the peace. The sky was so clear and blue and Mr. Sun had on his very best shine. Miss Mourning Dove gently cooed as she enjoyed the beginning of this lovely day. Madame Flutterby knew she must go outside and do something special on this perfect day.

" I know just where to go to begin my Hallelujah Day adventures...in the garden," she thought with a smile and off she went. She might go to the garden alone, but not for long. Soon she was joined by her dear friend Miss Lady Bug.

"What a wonderful day," she giggled. Miss Lady Bug was always giggling and finding happiness in everything she did. "Where should we go and what should we do on this cheerful day?" she asked.

"That's it! We should go find someone to cheer!" replied Madame Flutterby.

The two friends decided to visit and cheer Miss Shyleen Violet, who was new to the neighborhood. They had heard she was sick and needed someone to check in on her. On the way Madame Flutterby and Miss Lady Bug stopped to get some of Mrs. Dandy Lion's famous brewed tea. It was just the thing to help their new friend feel better. Mrs. Dandy Lion decided she would go along too.

"What a perfect day", she said. The friends agreed and off they all went on their adventure.

Feeling the warmth of the bright sunshine made the friends even happier and they began to sing. They sang about everything that made them happy. Miss Lady Bug started to giggle and before long they were all laughing.

While singing and laughing the friends passed the home of Mr. Given Inchworm. They heard a very loud voice holler, "Be quiet!" He was the grouchiest old worm in town. Startled for a moment, the friends were not going to let him spoil this wonderful day.

Cheerfully they greeted him and asked if he would like to join them? "We are going to visit Miss Shyleen Violet, she has been sick and we're bringing her some of Mrs. Dandy Lion's famous tea."

In a very grouchy voice Mr. Given Inchworm answered, "Why should I?" "No one ever comes to visit me and do anything nice for me." The friends were surprised by his answer and realized this might be why he was so grouchy.

"Please forgive us, we would like to be your friend and visit you, too." With that a smile came to Mr. Given Inchworms face and he thanked them.

They asked him to join them, knowing it would really help to cheer Miss Shyleen Violet to see all the new friends. He wanted to go but he felt he had nothing to share. Madame Flutterby smiled and explained he had the most important gift of all to share. Your gift is love and friendship. She is new to our garden and all alone.

They were right. When Miss Shyleen Violet saw the kind faces on the friends who came to visit, she was filled with joy.

While sitting and having tea together, they listened to her share some stories about herself and how glad she was to be living in the garden, especially now she has so many new friends.

Mr. Given Inchworm told her about his love of books and asked if he could read one of them for her. As he began to read the story, Miss Shyleen Violet settled in her favorite milkweed pod and quietly rested.

When the story was finished the friends knew it was time to go and let their new friend continue her rest. Giving her hugs, the friends said they would see her tomorrow and started home happily singing and laughing, even Mr. Given Inchworm. He laughed and said, "You were right, laughter and love are the best medicine, especially with friends. Thank you for showing me how important it is to care for those in need. I know now if I ever have a need I have lovely friends to call on for help." They hugged and waved goodbye until another day.

Arriving home Madame Flutterby smiles as she lay down in a Lily of the Valley leaf to rest. Closing her eyes, she smiles and gently speaks, "Thank You Lord, for this has been the most wonderful Hallelujah Day."

"Scriptures that inspired Miss Linda as she wrote the Hallelujah Day"

Matthew 22: 37-39   Love the Lord your God with all your heart and with all your soul and with all your mind....Love your neighbor as yourself.

1 Corinthians 13:13   And so faith, hope, love abide, but the greatest of these is love.

Psalm 20:14 May the words of my mouth and the meditation of my heart be pleasing in your sight, O Lord, my Rock and my Redeemer

Matthew 7:12   So in everything, do to others what you would have them do unto you

Revelation 19:1 Hallelujah!   Salvation and glory and power belong to our God

ABOUT THE AUTHOR

As a child, Miss Linda was able to express her imagination most vividly in the form of talking. Growing up in a home with 5 children, 2 parents and many animals, she wasn't always heard.

She found by going outside and hiding in the neighbors yards she could talk all she wanted and her imaginary friends would listen.   Birds, bugs and flowers became very special to her. Some of her favorites were butterflies, ladybugs and snapdragons.

Years later she discovered the talents of Beatrix Potter. Miss Potters writings and illustrations have had a big influence on Miss Linda all her life.

Miss Linda now writes and illustrates her stories with her own whimsical touch. Based on favorite scriptures, these enchanting, colorful tales will invite you into the wonderful Adventures of Madame Flutterby.